One, Two, Kangaroo

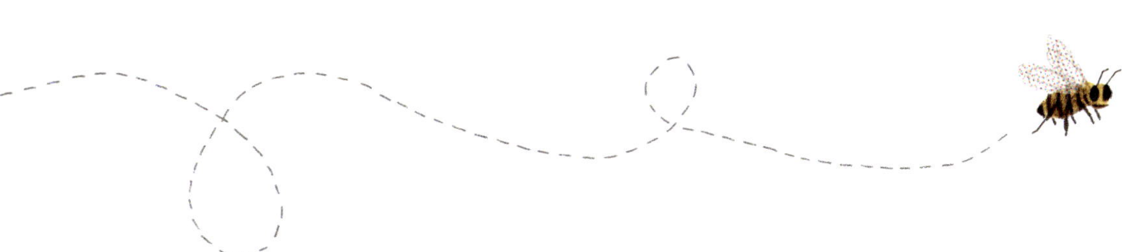

For Kirsten and Brian – CJ

Scholastic Australia
An imprint of Scholastic Australia Pty Limited
PO Box 579 Gosford NSW 2250
ABN 11 000 614 577
www.scholastic.com.au

Part of the Scholastic Group
Sydney • Auckland • New York • Toronto • London • Mexico City
New Delhi • Hong Kong • Buenos Aires • Puerto Rico

Published by Scholastic Australia in 2023.

Designed by Chad Mitchell.

A catalogue record for this book is available from the National Library of Australia

ISBN: 978 1 76129 008 4

Typeset in Josefin Slab.

Printed in China by RR Donnelley.
Scholastic Australia's policy, in association with RR Donnelley, is to use papers that are renewable and made efficiently from wood grown in responsibly managed forests, so as to minimise its environmental footprint.

10 9 8 7 6 5 4 3 2 23 24 25 26 27 / 2

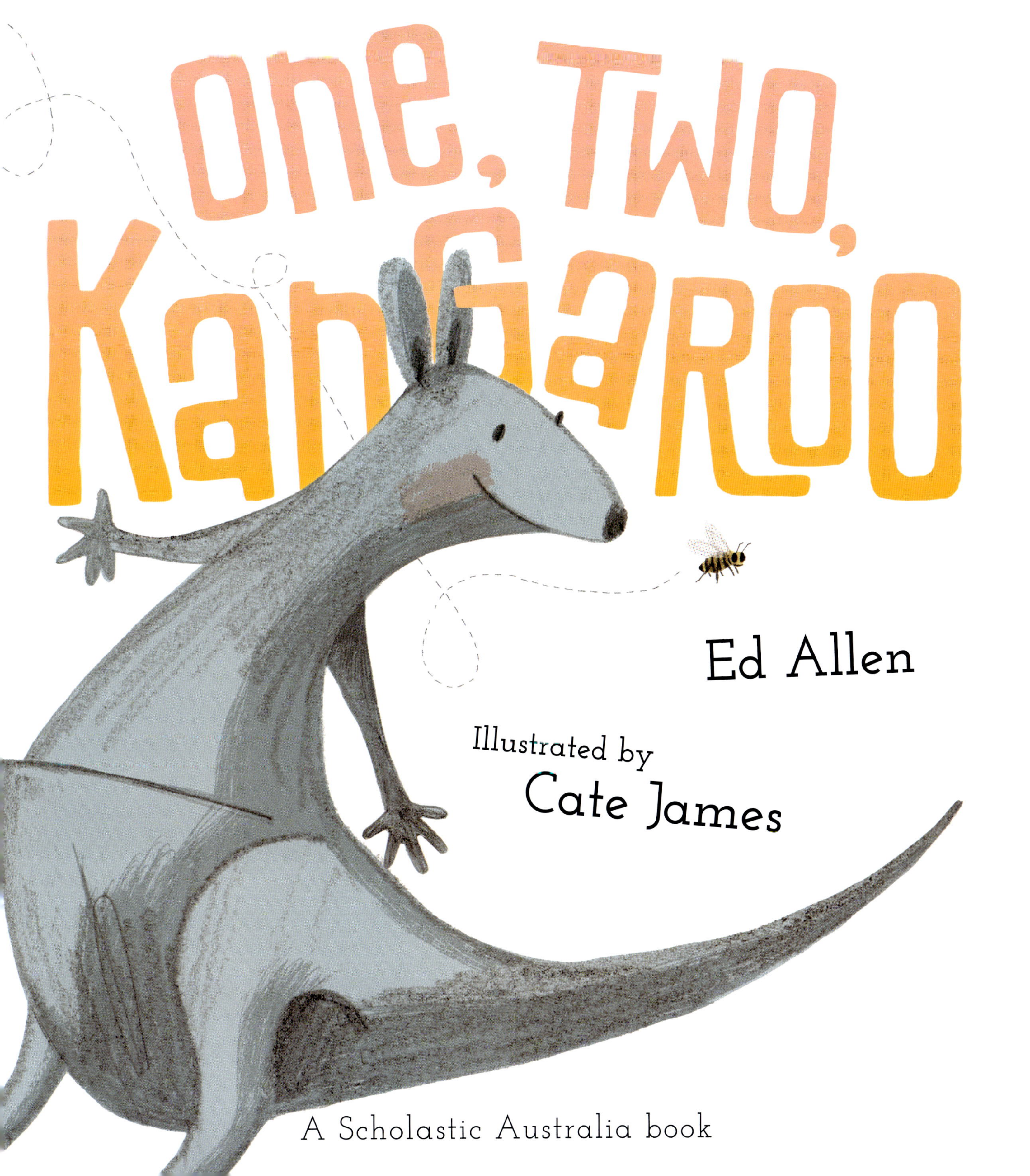
One, Two, Kangaroo
Ed Allen
Illustrated by
Cate James
A Scholastic Australia book

Way Down Under lives a giant kangaroo.
She has a long tail and a big pocket too!

How many friends can fit inside?
Let's see what happens. I'll go hide.

ONE little numbat, in the pouch of the roo.

Next makes TWO with a black cockatoo!

THREE with a croc,
down at the billabong.

FOUR with a possum
and her tail so long.

FIVE is a dingo, ‘Is there room for me?’

SIX is an emu, as you can see.

SEVEN, a goanna, it's becoming quite a crowd.
It's getting very squishy and it's getting very loud!

EIGHT is a flying fox, into the pouch too!

NINE is a lizard with his tongue so blue.

Is there room for one more?
It's just a teeny tiny bee.

WHOOPSIE!

EVERYBODY,

OUT!

TEN
NINE
EIGHT
SEVEN

SIX
FIVE
FOUR
THREE
TWO...

ONE.

Ten was too many! But as you can see,
the giant kangaroo always has space for . . .

ME!